3/2008

SCReWS

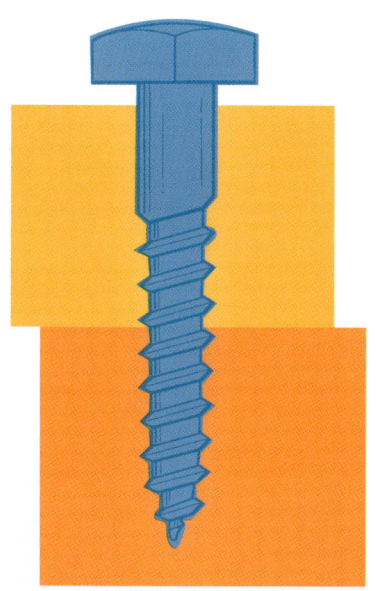

A Buddy Book
by
Sarah Tieck

VISIT US AT
www.abdopublishing.com

Published by ABDO Publishing Company, 4940 Viking Drive, Edina, Minnesota 55435.

Copyright © 2007 by Abdo Consulting Group, Inc. International copyrights reserved in all countries. No part of this book may be reproduced in any form without written permission from the publisher. Buddy Books™ is a trademark and logo of ABDO Publishing Company.

Printed in the United States.

Contributing Editor: Michael P. Goecke
Graphic Design: Maria Hosley
Cover Photograph: Photos.com, Clipart.com
Interior Photographs/Illustrations: Clipart.com, Corbis, Photos.com, Professional Litho, Stock Byte

Library of Congress Cataloging-in-Publication Data

Tieck, Sarah, 1976–
   Screws / Sarah Tieck.
      p. cm. — (Simple machines)
   Includes index.
   ISBN-13: 978-1-59679-817-5
   ISBN-10: 1-59679-817-3
   1. Screws—Juvenile literature. I. Title. II. Series: Tieck, Sarah, 1976- Simple machines.

TJ1338.T54 2006
621.8'82—dc22

2006010046

Table Of Contents

What Is A Screw? 4

Parts Of A Screw 8

How Does A Screw Work? 12

Different Screws At Work 14

The History Of Screws 18

**How Do Screws Help
   People Today?** 21

Web Sites 22

Important Words 23

Index 24

What Is A Screw?

Screws are used to hold things together. Screws also help lift and lower objects.

A screw is a simple machine. A simple machine has few moving parts, sometimes only one.

Simple machines give people a **mechanical advantage**. This is how screws help make work easier for people.

A corkscrew is a tool that helps open things such as wine bottles. People use corkscrews to pull out corks.

Screws are not the only simple machines. There are six simple machines. These include screws, wedges, pulleys, levers, **inclined planes**, and wheels and axles.

Sometimes, simple machines work together. Most machines are made up of more than one simple machine. Screws are found in many forms.

simple machines

Inclined Planes
Help move objects.

Levers
Help lift or move objects.

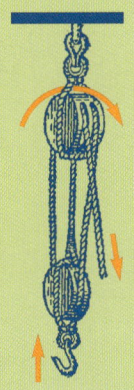

Pulleys
Help move, lift, and lower objects.

Screws
Help lift, lower, and fasten objects.

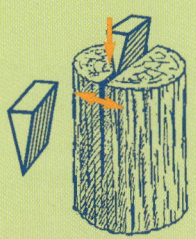

Wedges
Help fasten or split objects.

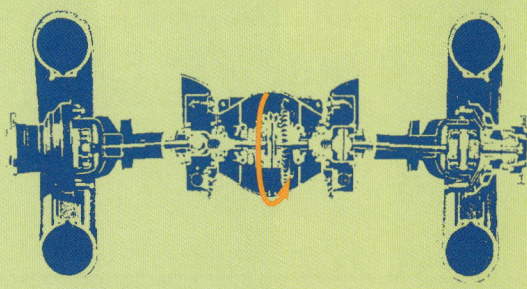

Wheels and Axles
Help move objects.

Parts of a Screw

Screws give people a **mechanical advantage**. The parts of a screw help fasten things together. Also, screws help people lift and lower things.

A screw is made up of an **inclined plane** wrapped around a **cylinder**. The inclined plane on a screw is called the **thread**. The thread drives the screw forward or backward as the screw is turned. The thread also helps the screw hold things together.

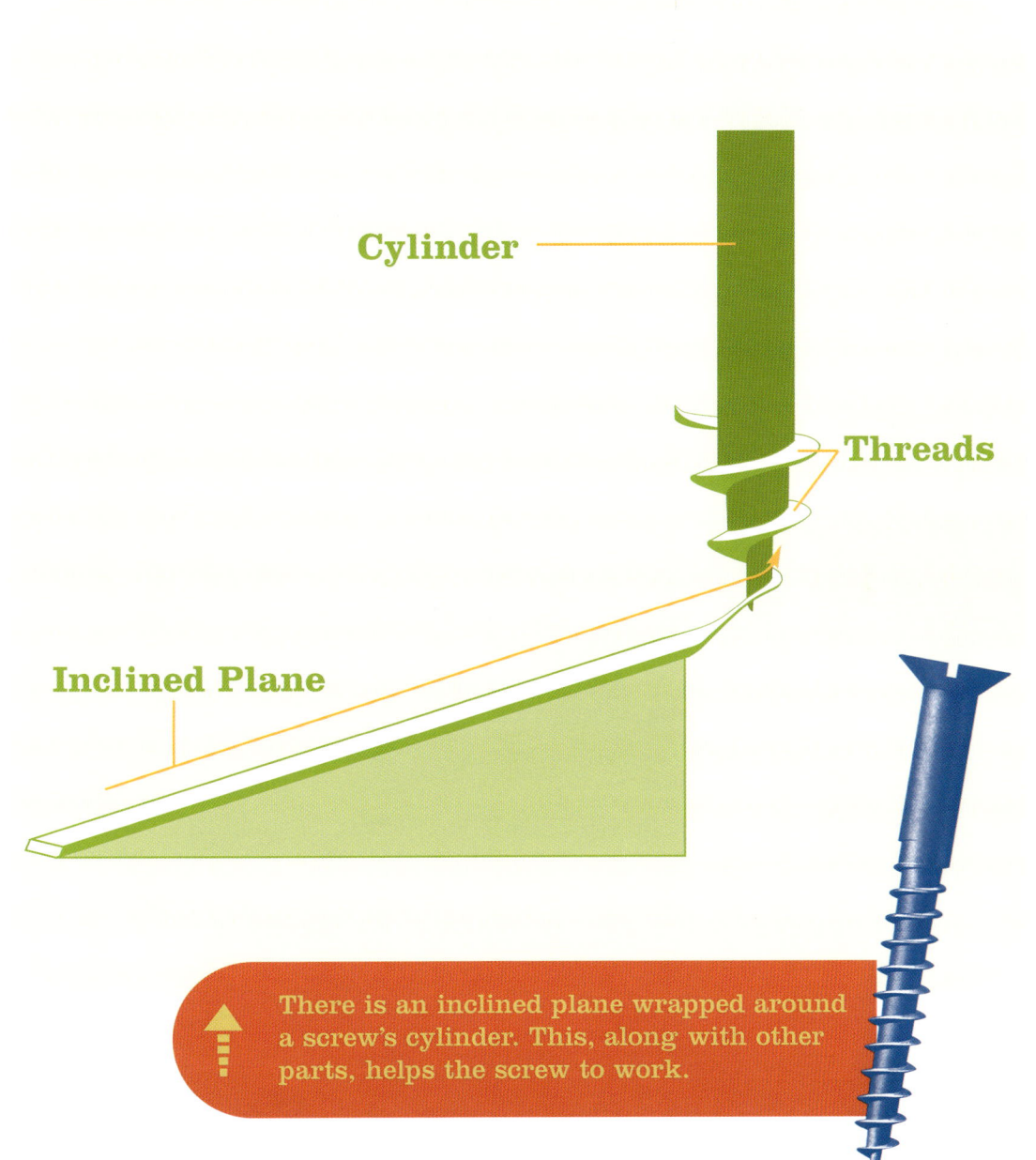

Cylinder

Threads

Inclined Plane

There is an inclined plane wrapped around a screw's cylinder. This, along with other parts, helps the screw to work.

Someone or something must supply **force** to turn a screw. This is how a screw fastens, lifts, or lowers an object. Often, people use another simple machine, such as a lever or a wheel and axle to turn a screw.

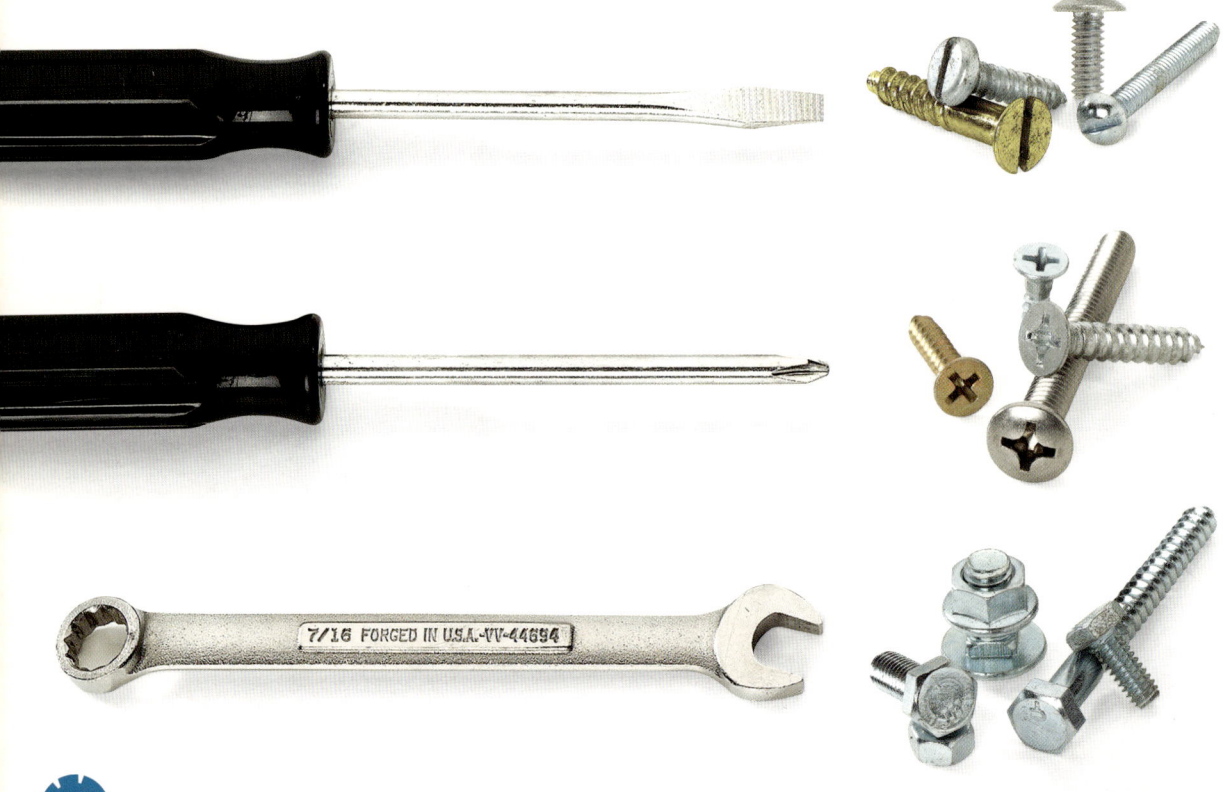

A wood screw helps to fasten things together. Many people use them when building things, such as decks.

A screwdriver is one tool that helps to turn a wood screw. People use a screwdriver to lift and lower the wood screw. The threads help it to do this.

How Does A Screw Work?

Screws make work easier. This is because a screw gives a person a **mechanical advantage**.

The lid of a jar is a screw. This screw is large and wide. Its **threads** are rounded and dull. This helps the lid fit onto the top of a jar.

When a person turns the lid and applies **force** the lid raises and lowers. This action helps fasten or unfasten the lid to the jar.

A jar's base has threads. So does the jar's lid. These threads fasten the jar and the lid together.

Different Screws At Work

There are many different ways to use a screw. It is possible to change a screw's shape, size, or **angle**. People can also change the way a screw moves. These changes help a screw to perform different jobs. Because of this, screws have many uses.

The base of a lightbulb is a screw. This screw is large and wide. Its **threads** are rounded and dull. This helps the lightbulb fit into a socket. When a person turns a lightbulb, it raises and lowers in the socket.

A lightbulb and a lightbulb socket.

This bar has threads.
When the bar is turned, it makes the jack lift or lower.

The sides are pulled together as the bar is turned.

 A jack is a tool that uses a screw to help lift objects. Jacks help people repair car tires.

A car jack also uses a screw. The screw helps the jack to raise and lower the weight of a car.

A car jack helps lift a car up and hold it in place. This lets people change a car tire.

The History of Screws

The screw has been used for many years. Greek mathematician Archimedes **invented** many machines using the screw. Archimedes and other Greek mathematicians helped people understand how to use screws to make work easier.

In early times, people didn't have machines with motors. They had to do work with their bodies.

The Archimedes Screw is a famous invention. It used a screw to lift and move water. It helped people give water to plants and animals.

These mathematicians were famous for their ideas. Each knew a lot about mathematics and science. They were always experimenting with formulas and theories.

Many times mathematicians discovered tools that helped people. Some of these tools and ideas are still used today.

How Do Screws Help People Today?

Today people have many types of tools, but they still use screws.

When you open a jar, you are using a form of a screw. When you use an adjustable wrench, you are using another form of a screw. When you put a key on a key ring, you are using yet another type of screw.

Keys and a key ring.

This nutcracker uses a screw to help crack a nut. The screw lifts or lowers when the handle is turned.

Screws help people with many different jobs all over the world.

Web Sites

To learn more about **Screws**, visit ABDO Publishing Company on the World Wide Web. Web site links about **Screws** are featured on our Book Links page. These links are routinely monitored and updated to provide the most current information available.

www.abdopublishing.com

Important Words

angle the shape made by two straight lines or surfaces meeting in a point.

cylinder an object that is shaped like a can of vegetables. The flat ends of a cylinder are circles.

force a push or pull against resistance.

inclined plane a flat surface that is raised at one end. This type of simple machine helps move objects to higher or lower places.

invent to create something that didn't exist before.

mechanical advantage the way simple machines make work easier. Using a simple machine to help with a task means less, or different, effort is needed to do a job. The same job would require more effort without the help of a simple machine.

thread the ridge that winds around a screw.

Index

adjustable wrench . . 21
Archimedes 18
Archimedes Screw . . 20
car jack 16, 17
corkscrew 5
cylinder 8, 9
deck 11
Greeks 18, 20
inclined
 plane 6, 7, 8, 9
jar 12, 13, 21
key 21
key ring 21

lever 6, 7, 10
lid 12, 13
lightbulb 15
mathematicians . . . 18, 20
nutcracker 22
pulley 6, 7
screwdriver 11
socket 15
threads 8, 9, 11, 12, 13, 15, 16
wedge 6, 7
wheel and
 axle 6, 7, 10